Cover illustration: Typical of the modern generation of 155mm self-propelled howitzers is the Italian OTO Melara Palmaria, which incorporates an extended 155mm barrel for greater range and an automatic loader for a higher rate of fire enclosed in a fully armoured turret on a high-mobility chassis. (OTO Melara)

1. The 155mm barrel of the OTO Melara Palmaria self-propelled howitzer is 41 calibres long and fires an HE shell to a maximum range of 24,000m. The system incorporates an automatic loader with a rate of fire of one round every fifteen seconds, and the vehicle carries 30 rounds with 23 ready to use in the automatic loader. (OTO Melara)

TANKS ILLUSTRATED No 18

Self-Propelled HOWITZERS

SIMON DUNSTAN

ARMS & ARMOUR PRESS
London New York Sydney

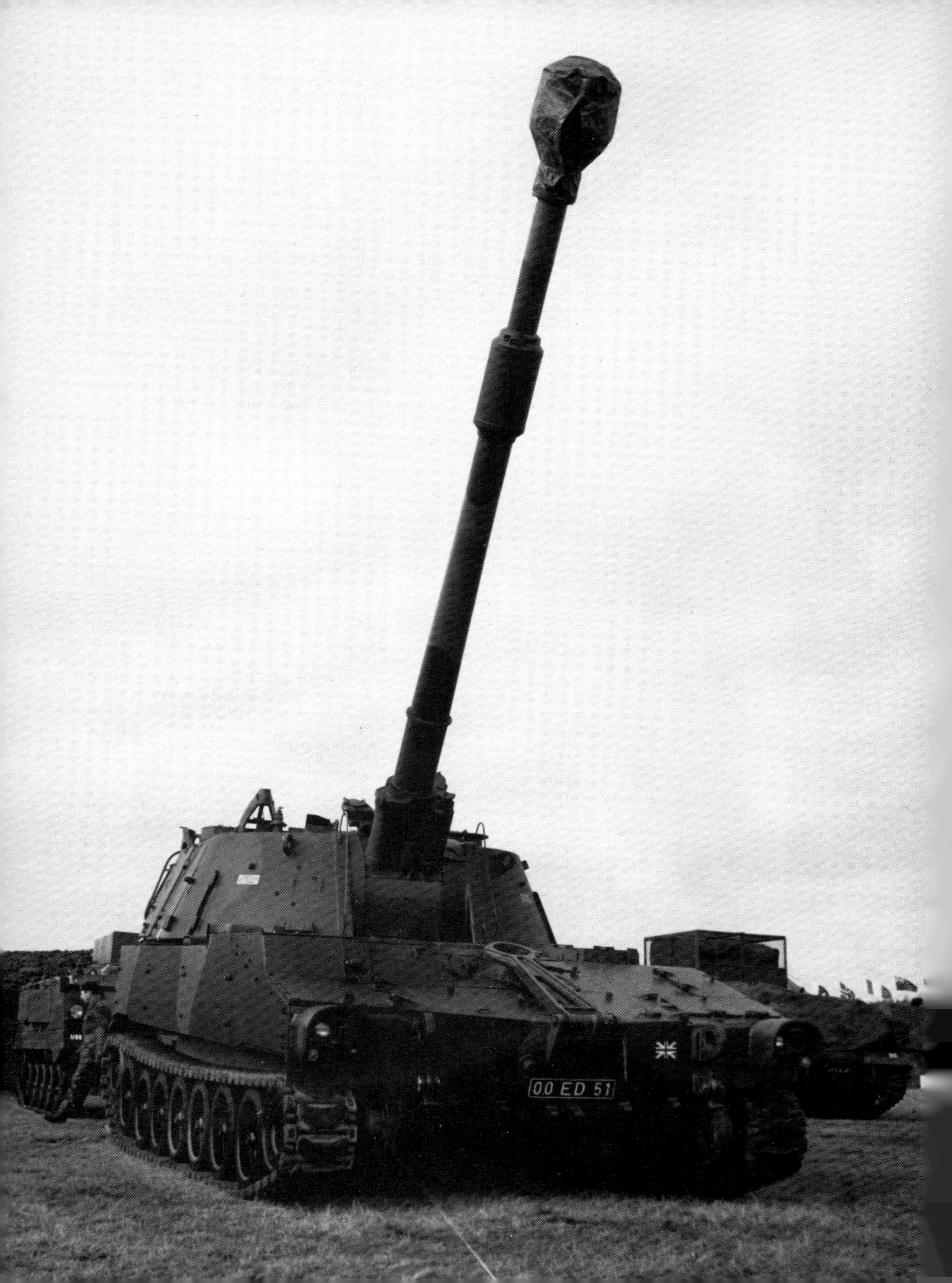
00 ED 51

Introduction

First published in Great Britain in 1988 by Arms and Armour Press Ltd., Artillery House, Artillery Row, London SW1P 1RT.

Distributed in the USA by Sterling Publishing Co. Inc., 2 Park Avenue, New York, NY 10016.

Distributed in Australia by Capricorn Link (Australia) Pty. Ltd., P.O. Box 665, Lane Cove, New South Wales 2066.

© Arms and Armour Press Ltd., 1988.
All rights reserved. No part of this book may be reproduced or transmitted in any form or by any means, electronic or mechanical, including photocopying, recording or via an information storage and retrieval system, without permission in writing from the publisher.

British Library Cataloguing in Publication data:
Dunstan, Simon, *1949 –*
Self-propelled howitzers – (Tanks illustrated: v.18)
1. Armoured combat vehicles: Tanks
I. Title   II. Series
623.74′752

ISBN 0-85368-765-X

Edited by Roger Chesneau; typeset by Typesetters (Birmingham) Ltd.; printed and bound in Great Britain by The Bath Press, Avon.

The role of field artillery remains predominant in the support of armoured and mechanized formations on the modern battlefield. Accurate and sustained fire support is vital both in the offence to suppress or destroy enemy troops, direct and indirect fire weapons, air defence systems and fortifications that might impede the advance, and in the defence of one's own positions during holding operations.

Today's artillery systems require both armour protection and mobility to survive on the battlefield and to support fast-moving mechanized units effectively. The majority of current designs feature a fully enclosed armoured turret mounted at the rear of a spacious tracked chassis, which affords protection against small-arms fire and shell splinters and provides sufficient room both for the gun crew to serve the weapon and for an adequate supply of ammunition for sustained and effective fire.

To fulfil its mission, the self-propelled howitzer can fire a wide range of projectiles. The majority of rounds fired are high-explosive, both ground and air burst, for the destruction of targets by blast and attrition, but also of great importance are smoke rounds to obscure friendly movements and illuminating rounds to deny the cover of darkness to the enemy. Other types include special-purpose projectiles such as nuclear, chemical, rocket-assisted or base-bleed rounds for engagements at extended range, precision guided munitions for pin-point targets, and scatterable bomblets or mines to impede the movement of enemy troops and armour.

With the advent of automatic or power-assisted loaders, high rates of fire can be achieved, providing saturation fire and/or a large volume of fire from one position before movement is necessary to avoid counter-battery fire. However, since most current SP howitzers carry only sufficient rounds for approximately fifteen minutes of firing, ammunition replenishment poses a significant problem, and several armies now employ specialized supply vehicles – some of which are based on the same chassis as the SP howitzer for maximum commonality – to sustain the artillery in the vast consumption of ammunition that characterizes the modern battlefield scenario. These vehicles are beyond the scope of this book, as are the multiple-launch rocket systems such as the M270 MLRS and the Soviet BM series, and ballistic missiles. *Tanks Illustrated No. 18* depicts a representative selection of the principal self-propelled artillery howitzers in use from the end of the Second World War to the present day.

The author wishes to thank those government departments, private companies and individuals that provided photographs for the compilation of this volume; in particular thanks are due to Public Relations MoD and United Kingdom Land Forces; Armscor; ECPA; the Royal School of Artillery; Kensuke Ebata; Christopher F. Foss; William Fowler; John Graber; K. Nogi; OTO Melara; Pierre Touzin; Urdan Industries Ltd; and Vickers Shipbuilding and Engineering Ltd.

Simon Dunstan

2. With its main armament at its maximum elevation of 75 degrees, a Royal Artillery M109A1 takes part in a display in Germany. The hull and turret are made of all-welded aluminium alloy to reduce weight, and the vehicle has a limited amphibious capability to negotiate rivers when fitted with inflatable air bags (which are not, however, normally carried on the vehicle). (MoD)

▲3 ▼4

3. At the close of the Second World War the United States and the Western Allies employed a wide variety of self-propelled guns and howitzers, the majority of which were based on the M4 Sherman chassis. In the final years of the war, the British Army used the Sexton mounting the 25pdr gun as its principal self-propelled artillery, and one is seen here on manoeuvres after the war near Stonehenge on Salisbury Plain. (MoD)

4. The '25-Pounder Self-Propelled Tracked, Sexton', as it was designated, was based on the chassis of the Canadian Ram tank (a derivative of the M4A1 Sherman), and 2,150 models were produced during the war at the Montreal Locomotive Works. Similar in configuration to the American M7 Priest, the Sexton incorporated the 25pdr gun instead of the 105mm howitzer for ease of logistical supply within the British Army. (MoD)

5. The Sexton remained in service with the British Army until 1956 but it continued to serve in other armies for many years thereafter, including those of India, Portugal and South Africa. Here a South African Sexton fires during a training exercise in the early 1970s. (SADF)

6. In the years immediately after the Second World War the French Army was equipped with predominantly American armoured fighting vehicles (AFV), many of which saw extensive service during the conflict in Indo-China. Here an M8 75mm howitzer motor carriage of the 1er Régiment de Chasseurs à Cheval returns fire during an ambush in Tongkin during 1952. (ECP Armées)

▲7 ▼8

7. With the outbreak of the Korean War in 1950, the US Army deployed numerous self-propelled guns and howitzers of Second World War vintage pending the introduction of more modern designs. Here M41 self-propelled howitzers of the 92nd Armored Field Artillery Battalion (SP 155) prepare to fire in support of advancing US Marine Corps infantry, 5 April 1951. (USMC)

8. Flying a Confederate flag, the crew of an M40 155mm self-propelled gun stand ready to support Marine operations during the Korean War. The M1A1 155mm gun was capable of firing a 95lb projectile to a range of 25,000 yards. (USMC)

9. An M40 155mm self-propelled gun of the 204th Field Artillery Battalion stands by the roadside as a precautionary measure near the demilitarized zone created at the conclusion of the Korean War in July 1953. (US Army)

10. Based on the chassis of the M4A3E8 (the final wartime M4 model), the M40 was the principal heavy artillery weapon of the armoured division and saw action from early 1945. A limited number of M40s were supplied to the British Army, but most of these remained in storage as a war reserve until declared obsolete in the early 1960s. (Royal School of Artillery)

▲11 ▼12

11. The first US postwar self-propelled artillery design to enter service was the M52 105mm self-propelled howitzer. The vehicle was first authorized in February 1948, and, owing to the demands of the Korean War, production began in January 1951 before trials had been fully completed. In consequence, the vehicle suffered numerous problems and it was not until December 1955 that the M52 was issued to field units. Based on the chassis of the M41 light tank, the M52 was one of the first SP artillery weapons to incorporate a fully rotating turret. (US Army)

12. After 1945, the British Army developed a light tank which was to be the basis for a series of vehicles including a 25pdr SP artillery gun, the FV304, but it never proceeded beyond the prototype stage. Subsequently, a design was proposed with the 25pdr mounted rearward on a Centurion tank chassis with only limited traverse left and right. This shortcoming, and the small size of the weapon in relation to the hull, posed serious limitations, and only two prototypes of the FV3802 were built. (MoD)

13. A further design based on the Centurion chassis incorporated a 5.5in gun with limited traverse in an armoured superstructure but, unlike the FV3802, the engine compartment was in the front. However, because of NATO's decision to standardize on 105 and 155mm calibres for artillery weapons, the FV3805 never entered production. (MoD)

14. Based on the same hull as the M52, the M44 155mm self-propelled howitzer was standardized in November 1953 and superseded the M41 howitzer motor carriage. Unlike the M52, the 155mm howitzer of the M44 was mounted in an open-topped armoured compartment at the rear of the vehicle with a traverse of 30 degress left and right. The M44 was widely employed by NATO armies and saw service with Belgium, Greece, Italy, Japan, Jordan, Spain, Turkey, West, Germany and the UK. (US Army)

15. In 1956, following the failure of the FV304, FV3802 and FV3805 and because of the near obsolescence of the Sexton, the British Army purchased two regiments of M44 SP howitzers to support the two armoured brigades serving in BAOR (British Army of the Rhine). Here, an M44A1 fires on the ranges at the Royal School of Artillery, Larkhill. The maximum range of the weapon was 14,600m. (Royal School of Artillery)

▲16

16. During the early 1950s, the US Army also produced two heavier self-propelled howitzers, the M53 and M55, which were based on components of the M48 medium tank. The M53 featured a 155mm weapon in a fully enclosed turret, thus overcoming the deficiency of the M44, while the M55 mounted an 8in howitzer. Illustrated is the M55, the full designation of which was 'Howitzer, Self-Propelled: Full Tracked, 8-inch, M55'. Both the M53 and M55 saw action in the Vietnam War with the US Marine Corps. (US Army)

17. With the NATO decision to standardize on 105 and 155mm calibres, the British Army opted for a self-propelled artillery weapon based on the FV430 series of tracked vehicles that were derived from the FV432 APC. Incorporating a new 105mm gun, the first of twelve prototypes of the FV433 was produced by Vickers in 1961. (MoD)

18. Following the Second World War tradition of naming self-propelled artillery weapons after ecclesiastics, the FV433 was named Abbot. The first production model was completed in 1964, and manufacture continued until 1967. (Author)

19. The Abbot design incorporates a fully rotating turret at the rear and the L13A1 105mm gun has a maximum elevation of 70 degrees and a depression of 5 degrees. Both movements are controlled manually while the turret traverse is powered. (MoD)

▼17

18▲   19▼

▲20 ▼21

22▶

20. Abbot is powered by a Rolls-Royce K60 multi-fuel engine with an Allison TX200 six-speed automatic transmission. Top speed is approximately 48kph and road range 390km. (Author)

21. Abbot's four-man crew comprises commander, driver, gunner and loader. Here a member of the 19th Field Regiment RA prepares to load a projectile into the breech. The weapon fires high-explosive (HE), high-explosive squash head (HESH), smoke and practice rounds. (MoD)

22. An Abbot of the 25th Field Regiment RA prepares to fire from a camouflaged position during a training exercise in West Germany. The maximum range of the gun is 17,000m and up to twelve rounds a minute can be fired. (MoD)

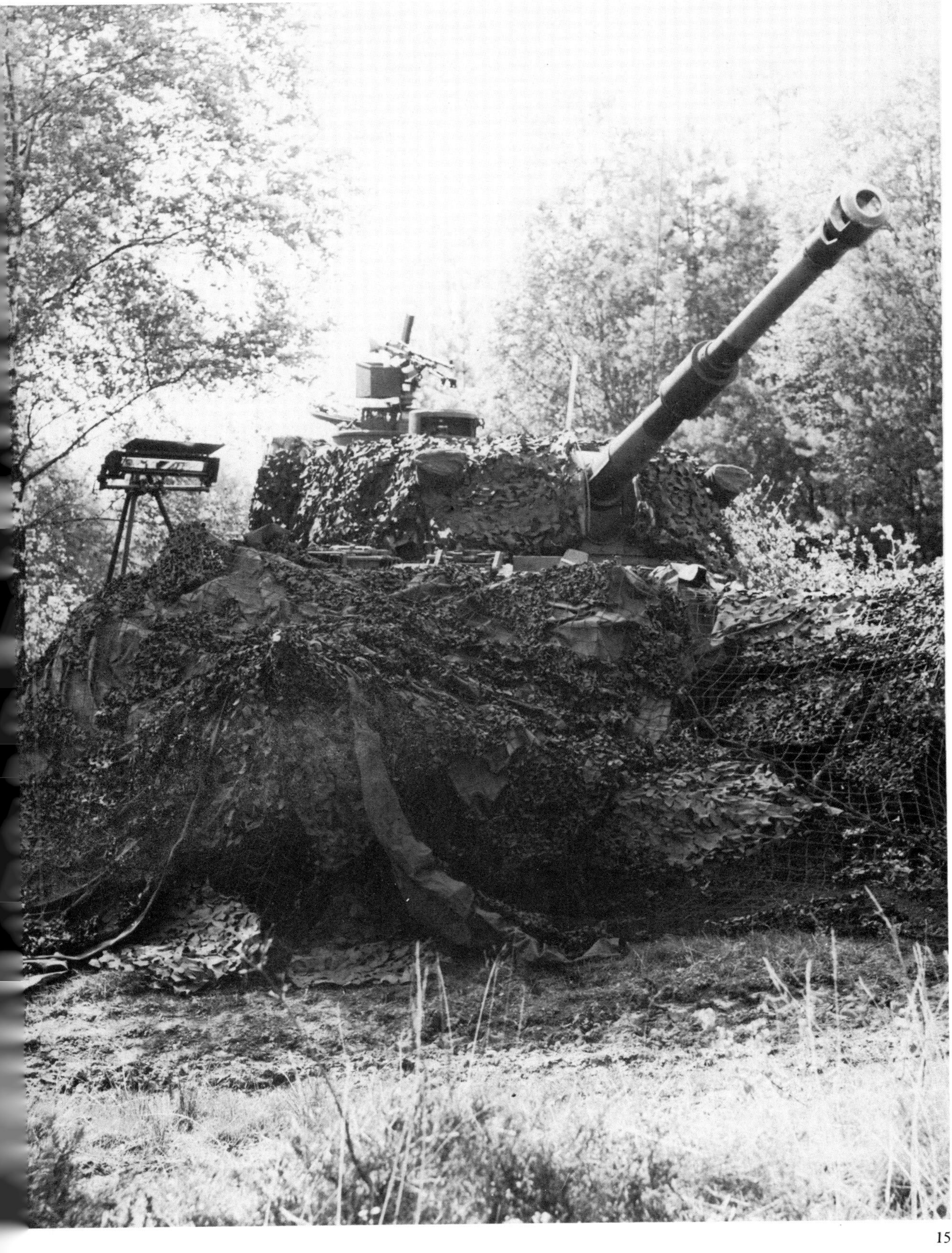

▲23 ▼24

25▲ 26▼

23. The Abbot can ford to a depth of 1.2m without preparation, and with the aid of a flotation screen it can swim inland waterways propelled by its tracks at a speed of 5kph. (MoD)

24. An Abbot's flotation screen is erected, a process which takes approximately 30 minutes. (MoD)

25. Festooned with typical camouflage, Abbots of the 25th Field Regiment RA negotiate a German village during Exercise 'Grosser Bär' in 1976. Forty rounds of 105mm ammunition are carried inside the Abbot, of which six are HESH to engage enemy MBTs in an emergency. (MoD)

26. The Abbot is employed by close support regiments of the RA and a regiment comprises four batteries each with six Abbots. The Abbot is currently due to be superseded in the British Army by 155mm-armed vehicles, but a simpler version known as Value Engineered Abbot remains in service with the Indian Army. (Vickers)

27. An FV433 Abbot churns up the mud as it negotiates a steep incline during manoeuvres in England. The vehicle weighs 16.5 tonnes, but the 240hp Rolls-Royce engine, the automatic transmission and the torsion bar suspension give Abbot an effective cross-country performance. (Author)

28. With communication wire running to the battery headquarters, an Abbot displays the NBC filtration equipment at the rear of the turret and the array of stowage boxes on the exterior of the vehicle to allow the maximum number of ammunition rounds to be carried under armour. (Author)

29. With guns in exact alignment, a battery of FV433 Abbots prepares to fire during a regimental shoot at the Royal School of Artillery, Larkhill. (Author)

28▲ 29▼

30. The Rt. Hon. Margaret Thatcher MP tries her hand at the controls of an Abbot of 40 Field Regiment RA during a visit to BAOR as leader of Her Majesty's Opposition, 23 January 1976. (MoD)

31. An ammunition handler prepares to load a shell into the breech of the 105mm gun of an Abbot at maximum elevation. The gunner and commander are seen in the background. (MoD)

32. In the depth of winter, a troop of Abbots conducts a firing exercise on Salisbury Plain. Although Abbot has a crew of four, an extra two members who act as ammunition handlers are normally carried on a support vehicle. (MoD)

33. Extensively camouflaged with bracken on the edge of a German wood, an Abbot takes up a position in the direct fire role against enemy armour which would be engaged with HESH ammunition – a tactic only used in the last resort. (MoD)

34. Despite the fact that SP artillery weapons normally remain well behind the front lines, they require a measure of self-protection from ground attack aircraft. Here, an Abbot is armed with an LMG, although in the light of the Falklands War experience shows that a .50-calibre machine gun is the minimum necessary for this requirement. (MoD)

32▲

33▲ 34▼

▲35 ▼36

35. The French equivalent of the Abbot is the 105mm Mk.61 self-propelled howitzer, or Obusier de 105 Model 50 sur Affût Automoteur. Based on the prolific AMX13 light tank chassis, it entered service in 1958 and production was undertaken by Atelier de Construction Roanne. (ECP Armées)

36. Two versions of the French 105mm SP howitzer were produced, one with a fixed fighting compartment and one with a fully rotating turret, as shown here. The latter was not adopted by the French Army but four were bought by the Swiss Army for trials purposes. (ECP Armées)

37. A 105mm Mk.61 self-propelled howitzer and another variant of the AMX13 light tank, the VTT/PC (Poste de Commandement), deploy into fire positions during manoeuvres in France. (ECP Armées)

38. The main armament of the Mk.61 is the M1950 105mm howitzer of 23-calibre length and it fires both an HE projectile to a maximum range of 15,000m and a high-explosive anti-tank (HEAT) round to engage AFVs. A total of 56 rounds of separate-loading ammunition (as shown) are carried on the vehicle, of which six are HEAT. (ECP Armées)

39. The Mk.61 has also been employed by the armies of Israel, Morocco and the Netherlands. The Dutch Army version incorporates a longer 105mm howitzer of 30 calibres and a commander's cupola with all-round observation periscopes. (Dutch Army)

40. A heavier artillery weapon based on the AMX13 is the 155mm Mk.F3 self-propelled gun, or Obusier de 155mm sur Affût Automoteur. The hull differs from that of the AMX13 and the Mk.61 in the deletion of the rear idler wheel, but because the vehicle is heavier than the tank it does not have the same cross-country performance. (ECP Armées)

41. The Mk.F3 has a crew of two with a driver and commander; the other eight members of the gun detachment are transported in another AMX13 variant, the VCA Véhicule Chenillé d'Accompagnement (or 155mm support vehicle), together with 25 projectiles, charges and fuzes. (ECP Armées)

42. With a maximum elevation of 67 degrees, the 155mm fires HE, illuminating and smoke rounds out to 20,000m plus a rocket-assisted projectile (RAP) to a maximum range of 25,300m. Over 600 Mk.F3 vehicles have been produced, and they have seen service with the armies of Argentina, Chile, Ecuador, France, Kuwait, Morocco, Qatar, Sudan, the United Arab Emirates and Venezuela. (ECP Armées)

41▲ 42▼

▲43 ▼44

43. Although the Mk.F3 was an effective and economical weapon system, its slow rate of fire and lack of armour protection for the gun crew led to its being superseded by the 155mm GCT self-propelled gun, GCT being Grand Cadence de Tir, or rapid-firing.
44. Based on the chassis of AMX30 main battle tank (MBT), the 155mm GCT entered service with the French Army in July 1979. The design incorporates a fully rotating turret with NBC protection and an innovative automatic loading system that permits a rate of fire of eight rounds a minute – twice that of the manually served Mk.F3 155mm.
45. The GCT's 155mm 40-calibre barrel has a maximum elevation of 66 degrees, and a total of 42 projectiles are carried in the turret, a typical ammunition load being 36 HE and six smoke, or 30 HE, six smoke and six illuminating rounds. The maximum range with a Brandt RAP round is 30,500m.
46. Deployed in artillery regiments, each of three batteries with six SP guns per battery, the GCT has superseded the Mk.61 105mm and Mk.F3 155mm models in the French Army and it is also employed by Iraq and Saudi Arabia.

47. Soon after the range of US self-propelled artillery pieces including the M44, M52, M53 and M55 had been accepted into the service, the US Army required the next generation of SP guns to be air-transportable and to feature common components to simplify logistics and reduce procurement costs. The Pacific Car and Foundry Company submitted designs for two SP weapons, the T235 175mm SP gun and the T236 8in (203mm) SP howitzer, which subsequently became the M107 and M110 respectively. They are shown here in British Army service. (Author)

48. The M107 features a 175mm M113 gun of 60-calibre length which allows long-range bombardment to a maximum distance of 32km, firing HE projectiles (M437A1 or A2) with a weight of 67kg containing 14kg of TNT. Here M107s of the 32nd Heavy Regiment RA fire on the ranges in West Germany. (MoD)

49. Production of the M107 was undertaken by the Pacific Car and Foundry Company from June 1961 and it entered service with the US Army in January 1963. The M107 was also produced by the FMC Corporation of San Jose and by Bowen-McLaughlin-York of York, Pennsylvania. (MoD)

49▼

50. An M107 175mm SP Gun of 'Q' (Sanna's Post) Battery of the 5th Regiment RA is prepared for action by its crew of eleven men, six of whom (driver, commander, layer and three loaders) are carried on the vehicle while the remainder are transported in a support vehicle which also carries the ammunition. (MoD)

51. The M107 is powered by an 8-cylinder Detroit diesel engine of 405hp coupled to a GM Allison Division XTG-411-2A cross-drive transmission giving a top speed of 56kph to range of 725km. (MoD)

52. The great length of the 175mm gun is shown to advantage on these brand new M107s which were procured by the British Army in 1965–66. The M107/M110 series has enjoyed considerable success in terms of sales and is in service with the armies of Greece, Iran, Israel, Italy, South Korea, the Netherlands, Spain, Turkey, the United Kingdom and West Germany (MoD)

53. The considerable size of the M107 makes it difficult to conceal in tactical positions, as evidenced by this example from 'P' Battery, 5th Heavy Regiment RA during Exercise 'Spearpoint' in West Germany during 1976. (MoD)

52▲ 53▼

▲54 ▼55

54. The M107 saw extensive service during the Vietnam War with both the US Army and US Marine Corps and, later, with the Army of the Republic of Vietnam. The guns were usually emplaced in fixed positions at fire support bases to cover wide areas of terrain, as demonstrated by this M107 of Battery 'A', 8th Battalion, 4th Artillery, at FSB Elliott during a fire mission on 20 July 1969. (US Army)

55. Besides their greater strategic mobility, one of the principal attributes of self-propelled artillery vehicles as compared with towed howitzers is the ability to move rapidly from one fire position to another, so as to avoid counter-battery fire. (MoD)

56. As part of the original design specification, the M113 175mm gun and M2A2 8in (203mm) are interchangeable, and the US Army has converted all its M107s to M110 models with an improved 203mm howitzer. The British Army is currently following suit, as are many NATO allies and the Israeli Army. (MoD)

57. Concurrent with the development of the M107/M110 series, the US Army sought replacements for the 105mm M52 and 155mm M44. Again, the new vehicle was to be air-transportable, but because of the smaller calibre weapons, the design was to incorporate full armour protection for the gun crew. The 105mm model was produced as the M108 self-propelled howitzer by the Cadillac Motor Car Division of General Motors during 1962–63, but only relatively few were built because the US Army stated its preference for the 155mm armed version, the M109. The M108, as illustrated, saw service with the armies of Belgium, Brazil, Spain, Taiwan, Tunisia and Turkey. (US Army)

▲58 ▼59

58. The M109 is almost identical to the M108 except for the main armament, fire-control system, ammunition stowage and the addition of large spades at the rear to provide stability during firing. The M109 entered service with the US Army in June 1963. Originally built by Cadillac and then by the Chrysler Corporation, the M109 is currently manufactured by Bowen-McLaughlin-York. (US Army)

59. The British Army first procured the M109 in 1965 and it serves with the Royal Artillery's medium self-propelled batteries in BAOR. The distinguishing feature of the M109 as against the M108 is the distinctive fume extractor and large muzzle brake of its M126 155mm howitzer. (MoD)

60. With a crew of six comprising commander, driver, gunner and three ammunition handlers, plus two others on a support vehicle, the M109 has a roomy fighting compartment. Here two ammunition handlers await orders to load an M109 of the 27th Medium Regiment RA during an exercise at Munsterlager. (MoD)

61. The gunner sits to the left of the weapon and is seen here adjusting the gun control equipment that incorporates an M117 panoramic telescope for indirect fire. Turret traverse and gun elevation/depression are hydraulically controlled, with a manual back-up for emergency use if the system becomes inoperative. (MoD)

▲62

62. The M109 has proved to be a most successful weapon system and is in service with the armies of 28 countries as well as the US Army and USMC. It is a rare example of NATO's ability to achieve standardization of equipment amongst its armies. Illustrated is an M109 of the Dutch Army. (Dutch Army)

63. The M126 155mm howitzer has a length of 23 calibres and is mounted in a fully enclosed, rotating turret on a seven-wheeled chassis; it is powered by the same engine and transmission as the M107/M110, which further enhances standardization. The vehicle has a top speed of 56kph to a maximum road range of 390km. This Danish M109 has its 155mm howitzer secured in the gun crutch for travelling. (Danish Army)

▼63

64. 'Charlie's Charmer', an M109 of the 11th Armored Cavalry Regiment, stands by for a fire mission against the VC/NVA at a fire support base in Vietnam during 1969. Although infrequently used in the mobile role, the M109 was widely employed to provide continuous artillery coverage to the infantry battalions operating in the jungles and paddy fields of Vietnam. Note the rear spades that were manually lowered to aid stability. (John Graber)

65. 'Congcoffin', an M109 of Battery 'C', 2nd Battalion, 138th Artillery, prepares to fire from Hill 88 in Vietnam, 19 March 1969. The M126 howitzer, firing the standard M107 HE projectiles weighing 42.9kg, has a maximum range of 14,600m. A total of 28 rounds of 155mm ammunition are carried in the vehicle, and the rate of fire is three rounds a minute. (US Army)

▲66 ▼67

66. Unlike the Abbot, the gunlayer of an M109 sits on the left of the 155mm howitzer (which is shown here with its breech open). The photograph gives an indication of the spaciousness inside the M109 as compared to the great majority of AFVs. (MoD)

67. The M109 displays the classic configuration of the modern SP howitzer with a stable, tracked chassis mounting a roomy turret set back on the hull which gives the maximum operating space for the crew and allows the rapid replenishment of ammunition through the rear doors. One of the most successful self-propelled howitzers, the M109 family has served many armies for almost 25 years; yet it remains the standard such vehicle by which other systems are judged. (Author)

68. From 1972 a new and longer barrel, designated M185, has been fitted to the M109 to give an increased range of 18,000m. Incorporating also improved elevation and traverse controls and a strengthened suspension system, vehicles so modified are designated M109A1. (Author)

69. The British Army began modifying its M109s to M109A1 standard during 1978. The barrel is of 39 calibres length and fires the same types of ammunition as previously but to a greater range, thus increasing the versatility and survivability of the weapon. (MoD)

70. The principal types of ammunition for the M109A1 are HE, smoke and illuminating rounds; others include nuclear, submunitions, chemical agents, rocket-assisted projectiles and precision guided munitions such as Copperhead, which is directed to the target by a laser designator. Here, an M109A1 of the Royal Artillery is prepared for firing, its long barrel masked by trees, during manoeuvres in West Germany. (MoD)
71. The commander of an M109A1 of the 45th Field Regiment RA observes the fall of shot during firing exercises on the Munster South ranges in West Germany. All M109s in British service have been modified to M109A1 standard and further new-build models, M109A2s, have been procured from the United States following the problems associated with the SP70. (MoD)
72. The difference in size between an Abbot and an M109A1 is readily apparent in this photograph. Both have proved to be effective artillery weapons with the British Army for over twenty years but are now in need of replacement. (Author)
73. The M109A2 is an improved version of the M109A1 incorporating several important changes, including a redesigned rammer and recoil system to increase the rate of fire, a roof-mounted armoured hood to protect the fire control optical equipment and a bustle at the rear of the turret to carry an additional 22 rounds of ammunition. The M109A2 entered service with the US Army in 1979. Each US Army armoured and mechanized division has three battalions of M109A1/A2s, each with three six-gun batteries, giving a total of 54 SP howitzers per division. (US Army)

72▲ 73▼

41

74. The companion vehicle to the M107 is the M110 8in (203mm) self-propelled howitzer. The first production vehicles were completed in 1962 by the Pacific Car and Foundry Company and entered service with the US Army in 1963. (MoD)

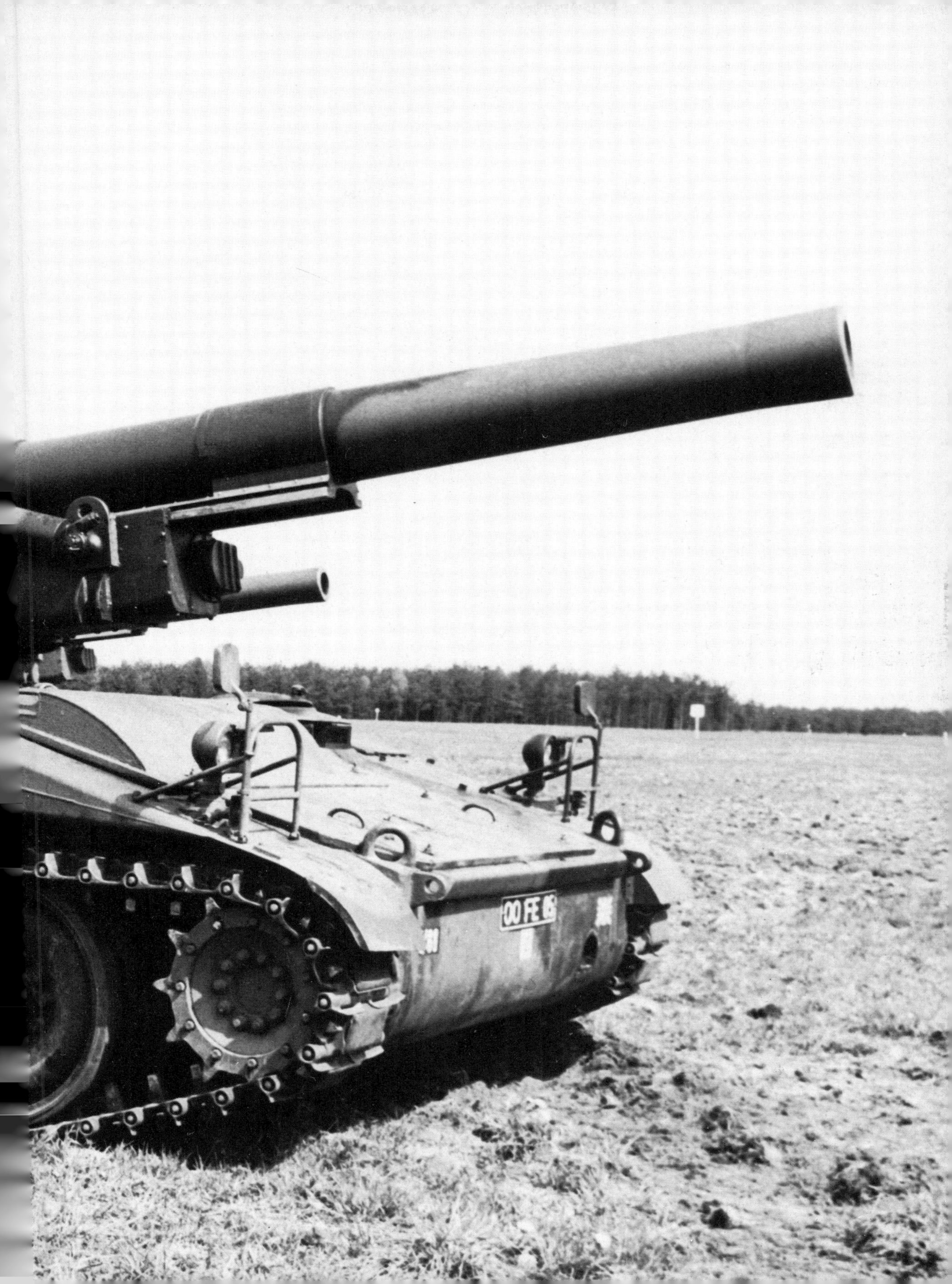

▲75
75. 'Alley-Oop', an M110 of the 3rd Battalion, 76th Artillery, and complete with Road Runner cartoon and the crossed cannon insignia of the Artillery Branch, prepares to move out during an exercise in West Germany. A battery of four M110s supports each US Army infantry division and a battalion of twelve supports each mechanized and armoured division. (US Army)

76, 77. The M107 and M110 share identical hulls and gun mountings, and their respective maximum ranges are 32,000m and 17,000m. All artillery weapons employ multi-charge propellants in any combination of up to eight charges, which allows targets to be engaged at varying ranges within the optimum trajectory. (MoD)

▼76

77▶

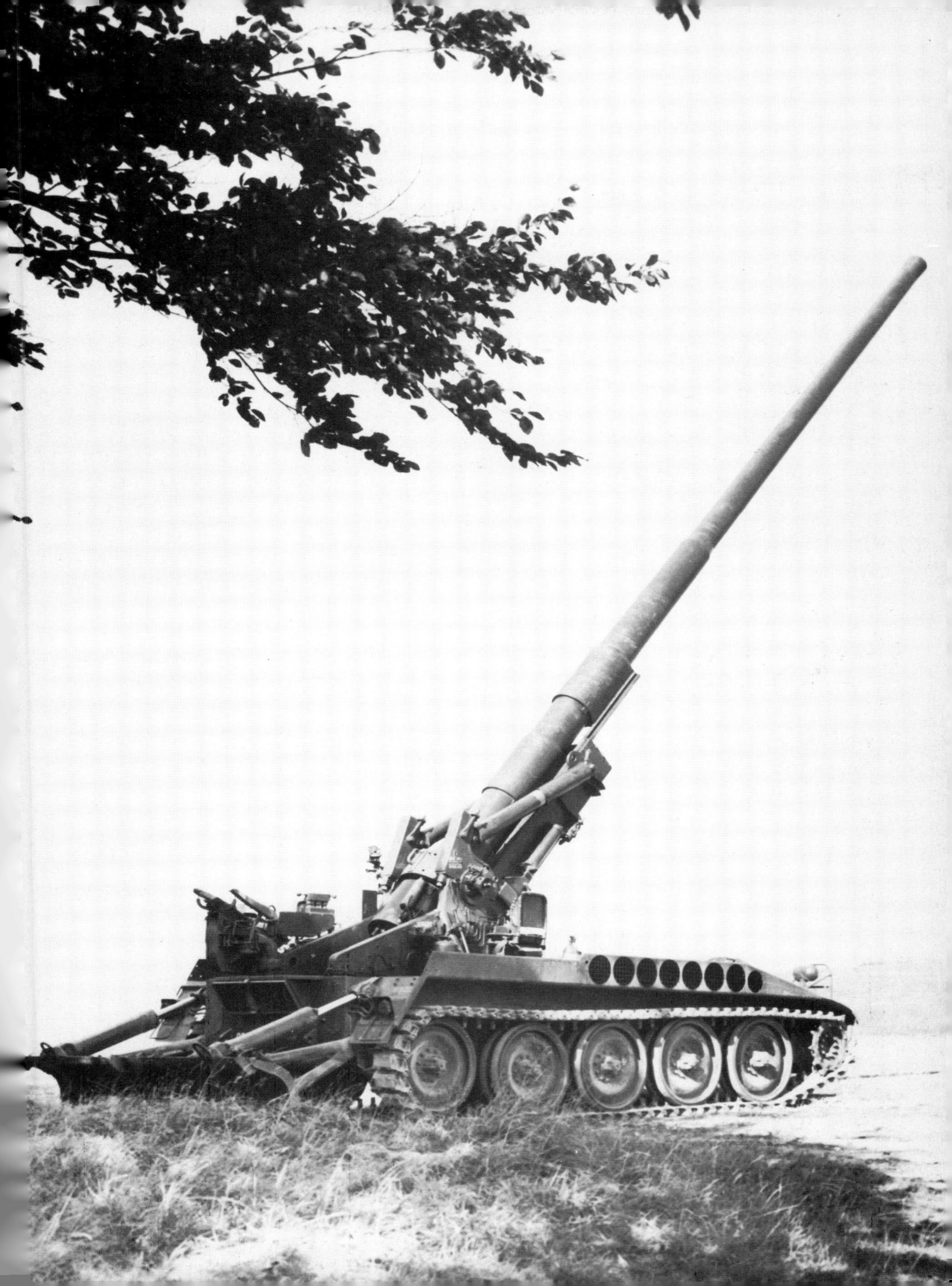

▲78
78. An M110 of 'H' Battery (Ramsay's Troop) of the 39th Medium Regiment RA is prepared for firing during training at Munsterlager in West Germany. Using 'shoot and scoot' tactics, M110s were employed operationally either singly or in pairs to fire nuclear projectiles from previously prepared positions and then move rapidly to alternative sites so as to avoid counter-battery fire. The British Army no longer retains a nuclear capability for its M110s. (MoD)
79. The M110 is in widespread service within NATO – here a West German battery fires during training – as well as numerous other armies, including those of Iran, Israel, Japan, Jordan, Saudi Arabia, South Korea, Pakistan and Taiwan.
80. The massive rear spade is raised after a fire mission by an M110 of the 27th Medium Regiment RA at Munsterlager. During firing, the vehicle's suspension is locked and the recoil shock is absorbed by the rear spade acting as an earth anchor. (MoD)
81. An M110 of the Royal Artillery moves off after firing. Six members of the eleven-man gun detachment travel on the vehicle, the remainder in a support vehicle which also transports the ammunition since only two rounds are carried on an M110. (MoD)

▼79

80▲ 81▼

▲82 ▼83

82. The breech assembly of an M110 illustrates the loading mechanism of a typical self-propelled howitzer with its hydro-pneumatic recoil system, interrupted screw breechblock and, behind the open breech of the 203mm (8in) M2A2 howitzer, the hydraulic rammer which also acts as a hoist to lift a 92.53kg HE projectile on to the loading tray prior to ramming it into the breech. To the rear of the vehicle is a large hydraulically operated spade which absorbs the recoil on firing. (Geoff Cornish)

83. Painted in the four-colour MERDC camouflage scheme, a US Army M110 is prepared for firing. The M2A2 howitzer fires M106 HE projectiles weighing 92.5kg to a maximum range of 16,800m as well as submunition, chemical agent and M422 nuclear rounds. The rate of fire is normally one round every two minutes but, for short periods, two rounds per minute can be sustained. (US Army)

84. The M110A1, an improved version of the M110 incorporating a longer barrel and a new range of ammunition, was introduced in 1977. The new M201 barrel increases the range when firing HE to 21,300m. Here an M110A1 trundles along a German road followed by its M548 support vehicle during a 'Reforger' exercise. (Pierre Touzin)

85. A subsequent modification in 1978 added a double-baffle muzzle brake to the end of the M201 barrel to allow a further increase in range by the use of Charge 9 propellant (the M110A1 being limited to Charge 8). The improved model is designated M110A2, and all M107 and M110 vehicles in US service are being modified to this standard. This M110A2 of 'A' Battery, 6/37th Field Artillery, is taking part in Exercise 'Team Spirit 86' near the Han River in South Korea. (US Army)

▲86
86. The first self-propelled artillery weapons of the Japanese Ground Self-Defence Force were thirty M52A1 and ten M44A1 SP vehicles which were procured from the USA in 1965. Subsequently an indigenous design, bearing a marked similarity to the British Abbot, was built, based on the automotive components of the Type 73 APC. Production of the Type 74 105mm self-propelled howitzer began in 1975, but only twenty were built because of a preference for a more effective 155mm model which became the Type 75. Here Type 74s are seen in service with the 2nd Artillery Regiment based at Asahikawa in the northern island of Hokkaido. (Kensuke Ebata)

87. First standardized in October 1975, the Type 75 155mm self-propelled howitzer is similar in layout to the M109 but features a Japanese-designed, 155mm, 30-calibre howitzer with a maximum range of 19,000m. On firing, the weapon automatically returns to an elevation of 6 degrees for reloading from two rotating magazines each holding nine projectiles and then returns to its original firing elevation. By this means, eighteen rounds can be fired in three minutes, while a further ten projectiles are carried in the vehicle. Approximately 200 Type 75s are in service with the JGSDF. (K. Nogi)

▼87

88. In keeping with its policy of neutrality and thus producing its own major weapon systems, the Swedish Army employs the 155mm Bandkanon IA self-propelled gun. Developed and produced by the Ordnance Division of AB Bofors, the vehicle was built in 1966–68 using components of the innovative S-tank (Stridsvagn 103), including the suspension, powerpack and transmission. (Swedish Army)

89. Mounted in the limited-traverse turret of 30 degrees, the Swedish 50-calibre 155mm has a maximum elevation of 40 degrees and fires a 48kg HE projectile to a maximum range of 25,600m. The hydro-pneumatic suspension is locked during firing to provide a more stable platform with no need for recoil spades at the rear. (Swedish Army)

▲ 90   ▼ 91

90. At 53 tons, the Bkv 1A is the heaviest AFV in the Swedish Army and lacks the high mobility associated with most of its vehicles operating in the hostile home terrain. Loading is achieved automatically from a fourteen-round magazine, which can be replenished from a supply vehicle by a jib mounted above the turret within two minutes. This system permits the remarkable rate of fire of fourteen rounds a minute – a figure which remains unmatched by any other SP weapon in service. (Swedish Army)

91. Developed in the late 1950s for the Israeli Army, the M50 155mm self-propelled howitzer comprises an M4A3E8 Sherman chassis mounting a French 155mm Model 50 howitzer firing a 43kg projectile to a maximum range of 17,600m. Here an M50 bombards targets in the Sinai Desert during the October War of 1973. (IDF)

92. The Soltam L33 155mm self-propelled gun/howitzer is based on an M4A3E8 Sherman chassis powered by a Cummins diesel engine and incorporates a 155mm M68 gun howitzer with a total traverse of 60 degrees in an enclosed superstructure. The Soltam L33 entered service with the Israeli Army in 1973 in time for the October War. (IDF)

93. Soltam have developed a 155mm self-propelled gun/howitzer turret, designated M72, that can be installed on MBT hulls such as the M48, the M60 or, as here, a modified Centurion. (Soltam)

94. The Israeli Army employs over 400 M109 SP howitzers and, in conjunction with the US Army, is currently developing an improved model, the M109A5. To enhance the vehicle's versatility and ensure a continuous supply of ammunition without resort to expensive support vehicles, Urdan Industries has developed the Artrail, which is a two-wheel trailer that is coupled to the SP in action or can be towed to its position by other vehicles such as a 5-ton truck or APC. The Artrail contains 44 rounds together with propellant charges and fuzes, and the ammunition is fed to the SP by means of a simple gravity system. The Artrail can be reloaded in fifteen minutes. (Urdan Industries)

▲95 ▼96

95. The OTO Melara Palmaria 155mm self-propelled howitzer was developed from 1977 specifically for the export market. It is based on the hull of the company's OF-40 MBT, and the first production vehicle was completed in 1982. The Palmaria has been purchased by Libya and Nigeria. (OTO Melara)

96. Until the 1970s the Soviet Army possessed no self-propelled howitzers, but following a radical modernization of its conventional artillery branch it now possesses a range of SP weapons comparable in calibre and capability to those of the NATO nations. The SO-152 Akatsiya 152mm self-propelled howitzer appeared in 1972. It has a six-man crew and can fire an HE projectile to a range of 17.3km at a rate of fire of three rounds a minute.

97. SO-152 Akatsiyas trundle through Red Square during a military parade. The Akatsiya (Acacia) mounts a D-20 152mm and shares the same chassis as the SA-4 'Ganef' air defence missile system. The Soviet Army has also fielded two self-propelled guns, the 2S5 and 2S7, that fulfil the same roles as the M107 and M110.

98. To replace the towed D-30 122mm howitzers in its motor rifle and tank divisions, the Soviet Army employs the SO-122 self-propelled howitzer Gvozdika (Carnation). The vehicle is amphibious and fires an HE projectile to a range of 15.2km. It is deployed in battalions of three batteries with six vehicles in each, a front-line tank division having six battalions totalling 108 vehicles.

97▲ 98▼

▲99   ▼100

99. While the SO-122 and SO-152 are now deployed in several Warsaw Pact countries, the Czechoslovak Army has developed an unusual 152mm self-propelled howitzer based on the eight-wheeled Tatra 813 heavy truck. Designated the 152mm VZ.77 DANA (Delo Automobilny Nabijene Automatickly), the weapon incorporates an automatic loader with a high rate of fire. The vehicle is also in service with the Libyan Army.

100. The South African Defence Force (SADF) also deploys a wheeled 152mm self-propelled howitzer, which is known as the G6 Renoster or Rhino. The advantages of the wheeled configuration are greater strategic mobility to cover the long distances in the particular theatre of operations faced by the SADF, reduced maintenance and operating costs, and a similar cross-country performance to the Ratel Infantry Fighting Vehicle, the principal SADF AFV for counter-insurgency warfare and with which the G6 has been designed to operate.

101. At 46 tonnes, the Renoster is the largest wheeled artillery vehicle in the world. Well armoured against its principal threat, land mines, the G6 has a crew of five, with the driver located in a separate compartment forward of the engine and behind an armoured wedge-shaped box that acts as a bush-clearing device as well as containing sixteen projectiles. (Armscor)

102. A Rhino in its natural habitat – the bush – where the vehicle's speed is in excess of 30kph; on roads its maximum speed is at least 85kph. With a fuel capacity of 700 litres, the G6 has a range of 600km at an average speed of 80kph. In and out of action times are a remarkable 60 and 30 seconds respectively, while a firing rate of three rounds per minute with the maximum charge can be achieved for a period of fifteen minutes. The secondary armament comprises a 12.7mm machine gun, eight 81mm smoke grenade launchers and four firing ports for the crew's personal weapons. (Armscor)

▲ 103
103. The G6 Artillery System incorporates a 45-calibre 155mm howitzer with an elevation range of −5 to +70 degrees. It fires a wide range of projectiles to a maximum range of 39,000m, including a high-performance HE round, WP and a series of cargo projectiles that dispense incendiaries, propaganda leaflets or submunition bomblets for anti-armour and anti-personnel applications. The G6 carries 47 projectiles and 52 propellant charges. The vehicle can be fully replenished by three crew members within fifteen minutes; for continuous firing, ammunition is fed by chute through the rear doors from a Ratel logistic support vehicle. (Armscor)

104. While not strictly self-propelled artillery, the FH70 155mm howitzer does illustrate the tendency of modern towed artillery pieces to embody a degree of mobility by means of an auxiliary engine, enabling the weapon to manoeuvre into and out of fire positions as well as, to a limited degree, cross-country. (MoD)

▼ 104

105. Concurrent with the development of the tri-national FH70 towed 155mm howitzer, a self-propelled version, the SP70, was proposed. The West Germans were to be responsible for the chassis, using components of the Leopard 1 and 2 MBTs and the Marder MICV, the British for the turret and automatic loader and Italy for various other aspects of the vehicle.

106. A West German SP70 fires during trials, with the shell replenishment gear deployed at the back of the turret. While much of the SP70 embodies components from other proven systems, the automatic loader has failed to meet the design specification of firing three rounds in ten seconds and six rounds per minute and, in consequence, the project was cancelled in 1986. The three countries were thus left with an urgent requirement for a modern SP howitzer.

107. One of the contenders to replace the British Army's ageing 105mm Abbots is the Artillery System 90 or AS90. A joint venture between VSEL (Vickers Shipbuilding and Engineering Ltd.) of Britain, the Cummins Engine Company of the USA and Verolene Estaleiros Reunidos do Brazil, the AS90 is a cost-effective system that can be configured to many degrees of sophistication to meet customer requirements. (VSEL).

108. Using proven components wherever possible, such as the same engine as the M2/M3 Bradley and the M270 MLRS (Multiple Launch Rocket System), the same gun as the FH70 and a hydrogas suspension derived from that of the Challenger MBT, the AS90 has been designed on a modular basis so that future technological developments can be accommodated without extensive reworking. For example, the AS90 can accept 155mm gun barrels up to 52 calibres in length without modification to the recoil system. (VSEL).

109. With a 39-calibre barrel, the AS90 has a range of 24,700m and can fire three rounds in ten seconds or six rounds per minute for a short period. A total of 40 projectiles are carried, and all NATO 155mm ammunition – plus many other types such as precision guided munitions and extended range rounds – can be fired. With a wide range of optional equipment such as computer-based gun-laying and inertial navigation, AS90 represents a most versatile design. (VSEL)

▲110

110. Royal Ordnance is also competing for the British Army's replacement for Abbot, with a version of the M109 to be built in conjunction with the US parent company, BMY. The two companies are also competing in a requirement of the Arab Republic of Egypt for a self-propelled artillery vehicle mounting a Soviet 122mm D30 howitzer. The BMY model is based on the M109 (see *Tanks Illustrated 26*, photograph 25), while the Royal Ordnance model mounts the weapon on the chassis of the RO2000 family of tracked AFVs. (Royal Ordnance)

▼111

111. Besides the AS90, Vickers Shipbuilding and Engineering also produce the GBT 155mm Universal Turret, which can be fitted to a wide variety of MBT hulls (in this case Challenger) to provide a self-propelled howitzer at minimum cost, especially when using the chassis of an otherwise outdated tank. The turret is self-contained and requires no power from the chassis. The main disadvantage of such a system is the height of the vehicle for ammunition replenishment, which is through the rear of the turret. (VSEL)

112. In order to augment its 105mm Abbots and increase its SP artillery capability, the Indian Army is considering the GBT 155 mounted on the chassis of the Vijayanta, a locally produced version of the Vickers Mk. 3 MBT, as shown here. The turret can be fitted to virtually any chassis that is able to absorb the recoil forces on firing, including the T54/55, M48/60, Centurion and Leopard. (VSEL)

113. A GBT 155 turret is mounted on the hull of an M109 to test the validity of the system on a lighter chassis than that of an MBT. When firing standard ammunition, the GBT 155 has a range of 24,700m or, with extended-range ammunition, 32,000m. (VSEL)

▲114 ▼115

114. The world demand for modern self-propelled howitzers remains constant, and manufacturers are continually introducing further improvements to their products to suit particular customers. The M109 family for example, is being developed to ensure its effectiveness into the twenty-first century. The latest model, which is to be type-classified as the M109A5, is a result of the Howitzer Improvement Program or HIP (see *Tanks Illustrated No 26*). A further conceptual development is the M109 Maxi-PIP New Turret (shown) which incorporates the semi-automatic handling and loading of ammunition, increased range and rate of fire, improved accuracy and many other features. (FMC)

115. To meet the US Army's requirement for a future self-propelled howitzer known as the Division Support Weapon System (DSWS), FMC have proposed a further development of the M109 on a lengthened chassis with a fully automatic loading system, so reducing the number of crew members required but permitting a greatly increased rate of fire with a multiple-target capacity. (FMC)